An Affair of the Stilled Heart

An Affair of the Stilled Heart

Bobby Aldridge

LITERARY PRESS
LAMAR UNIVERSITY

ISBN: 978-1-942956-18-1
Library of Congress Control Number: 2016936028

Cover Photograph: Ashley Valentine Young
Manufactured in the United States

Lamar University Literary Press
Beaumont, Texas

For those who wait for me
and those I will await

Poetry from Lamar University Literary Press

Charles Behlen, *Failing Heaven*
Alan Berecka, *With Our Baggage*
David Bowles, *Flower, Song, Dance: Aztec and Mayan Poetry*
Jerry Bradley, *Crownfeathers and Effigies*
Jerry Bradley and Ulf Kirchdorfer, editors, *The Great American Wise Ass Poetry Anthology*
Matthew Brennan, *One Life*
Paul Christensen, *The Jack of Diamonds is a Hard Card to Play*
Christopher Carmona, Rob Johnson, and Chuck Taylor, editors, *The Beatest State in the Union*
Chip Dameron, *Waiting for an Etcher*
William Virgil Davis, *The Bones Poems*
Jeffrey DeLotto, *Voices Writ in Sand*
Mimi Ferebee, *Wildfires and Atmospheric Memories*
Larry Griffin, *Cedar Plums*
Ken Hada, *Margaritas and Redfish*
Michelle Hartman, *Disenchanted and Disgruntled*
Michelle Hartman, *Irony and Irreverence*
Katherine Hoerth, *Goddess Wears Cowboy Boots*
Lynn Hoggard, *Motherland*
Gretchen Johnson, *A Trip Through Downer, Minnesota*
Ulf Kirchdorfer, *Chewing Green Leaves*
Laozi, *Daodejing*, tr. By David Breeden, Steven Schroeder, and Wally Swist
Janet McCann, *The Crone at the Casino*
Erin Murphy, *Ancilla*
Laurence Musgrove, *Local Bird*
Dave Oliphant, *The Pilgrimage, Selected Poems: 1962-2012*
Kornelijus Platelis, *Solitary Architectures*
Carol Coffee Reposa, *Underground Musicians*
Jan Seale, *The Parkinson Poems*
Carol Smallwood, *Water, Earth, Air, Fire, and Picket Fences*
Glen Sorestad *Hazards of Eden*
W.K. Stratton, *Ranchero Ford/ Dying in Red Dirt Country*
Wally Swist, *Invocation*
Jonas Zdanys, *Red Stones*
Jonas Zdanys (ed.), *Pushing the Envelope, Epistolary Poems*

For information on these and other Lamar University Literary Press books go to
www.Lamar.edu/literarypress

Acknowledgments

"To Plait Celestial Chains" previously appeared in *Society of Classical Poets* Feb 2013, edited by Evan Mantyk

"Childhood" previously appeared in *Poetry Quarterly* Fall 2015, edited by Glenn Lyvers

CONTENTS

Lower case listings are untitled poems.

Consolation

We carefully plant each other in broad fields,
or in pots on marble shelves and mantles,
to hopefully await the harvest.

Even the most faithful of us rarely claim to know well
the shadowy provinces to which we journey.

Sometimes as children we fear the dark,
playing hide-and-seek to confront our fears.
Sometimes as adults we fear the dark,

stand with our back to the veil pretending not to notice.
We feel trepidation at corners around which we cannot see.

We find consolation in religion and fond memories
held by those left behind, religion in kind words spoken,
the most distant memories aroused by those recently come.

* * *

Still, we watch for specters in the night,
we entertain misty doubts and faithless fears
in whispered stories and cautionary tales.

Death is a teacher of discipline and introspection,
a skull on the post to warn others of what waits,

the distilled essence of political power over the solitary heart,
the consummate companion in foolhardy endeavors.
It keeps children from streets, and young girls from strangers.

Perhaps the way we address death, more than anything else,
defines us as civilized and cognizant beings.

From funeral pyres, to burials at sea, to the tower of silence,
we either shun the dead or affirm our closeness to them.
Before any god's judgment, any faith, are the funerary rites.

* * *

It is the confirmation of otherwise hollow faith.
It is the recognition of our physical form.

We send recommendations with souls to the afterlife.
We inscribe introductions on marble and granite.
Though paradise may not be claimed incontrovertible,

it is implied, as we consecrate carefully crafted vessels
and dress travelers for their ceremonious reception.

We acknowledge the continuation of existence in memories.
We reach across the gulf, hold loved ones by their legacies.
Death is the one universal.

The myriad reflections and emotions associated with death,
and dying, and waiting to die are common to all.

Verses or prose, songs or dirges, follow and explore our lives
and our relationships, our fascinations and fears.
We honor shared humanity and disinter collective reverence.

Strength in Numbers

I am a mighty locust.
I was meant to be a part of a huge swarm,
to desolate the earth in my wake.
But separated,
no matter how I struggle,
bureaucratic ants divide me,
flightless,
I am carried away altogether.

Reach

Dancing in the wind,
arms outstretched toward destiny,
ponder my future.

      Clear from scenic overlook,
      see me fall from the guard rail.

Acrostic Abel

Abel ate apples
bit by bit.

Cane's concealed core,
down deep,
eat everything ecumenically,
finding fault   fruitless,
gave God's good grace
hard-hearted hatred.

* * *

In ignominy interred,
just,
kind King,
lamented
man.

* * *

Now night
obfuscates our
pure purpose,
quintessent,
redemptive
son.

Taken tragically,
undeserved.

* * *

Vexed, voracious
wonton, wolves, wasting.

Xeric
yoke, yields
Zechariah's zenith.

The Constant Earth

Has it not always been the good earth
    that has received us?
The good earth
    that bore the warhorse and the soldier?
The good earth
    that held fast the great oak and the insidious vine
And at last is it not the good earth
    that cradles our head as we sleep?

She has born the soles of dancers and vagabonds
    and fed them by the way.
She has received the pleasures of farmers
    and nursed their young.
She has adorned herself with flowers and jewels
    when we have courted her in a new place.
She is pulled up close around us
    as we crawl in frightened of the night.

And for her noxious herbs
    we have cursed her.
And for her stony soil
    we have lamented our affair.
From the garden she has kept her part,
    thistles matted in her hair.
And from the garden has she received us into her heart
    as we return from our errant ways.

Decay

An ageing athlete, the old carpenter spoke
in an unending stream of obscene clichés,
witty stories, lewd jokes, terms of endearment,
dust to dust, not a long journey.

Kanshi for Late Autumn

I lay dozing, dreaming, a western land,
a paradise, I lack a better term.
She mops my face with a cloth,
reassuring me, I don't have to go.

Traveling in the Fog

There are places that we would fit, that we would never go.
They are close at hand. I see them in the corner of the room
or the grass at the base of the tree.
I stand or walk by, but I never go down there.
They deliberately make places like that,
chairs on landings or in hallways,
rails on rooftops or parapet walls,
ladders up the sides of towers.
These are quiet places that want visiting.
I would have as a child. I did.

If I could just slow down...
You can't imagine how long it's been
since I looked at the sky.
I mean really laid in the grass and stared,
imagining where it could lead,
what clouds must feel like when you get on the solid ones.
Then I would remind myself that the concept is foolish.
I know how clouds feel from misty mornings.
Still, I think the journey was of value.

When they come in and discover me under the desk
or exploring the ecosystem of the carpet
as though I could walk around between the fibers
and find buried treasure in the coarse woven soil,
will I need a home?
Is that senility?
Is that Alzheimer's?
Did my grandmother just start noticing the details,
seeing the small spaces?
Did she remember her childhood too well?
Was that easier than the present, right after he died?

What if I lie in the grass too long and discover
the roots of the huge oak tree for what they could be?

Patient

Whispering to me,
the old general told stories,
while I cleaned his wound,

>not wanting to wake the ward,
>dozing in the afternoon.

Dragonflies swiftly
glide low over still waters
recall days as nymphs.

>The man asked if I'd seen her
>but Mary's been dead ten years.

Restrained and sobbing,
he spoke as if I knew him,
asking to go home.

>Calling from a western land
>snow crushing the old hawthorn.

Has Jake gone to bed?
She asked the night nurse passing,
calling her Alice.

>Late frost collects in the sill,
>rotting wood swells, jams the sash.

The snow settles in,
filling the panes of windows,
long since painted shut.

>Children come for holidays
>to comfort pathetic souls.

An ill fitting life
gnarled, brittle, thick grey bark
fighting coming dark.

    Early autumn, already
    thinking of the first snowfall.

Daedalus

I was a powerful man in my youth,
understanding clearly the engines of war,
seeing clearly the movements of the seasons.

I was a great teacher.
The children at my knee offer to carry my load.
They try to take my hand to lead me on my way.

I stood before kings before they could stand.
I still see clearly the movements of seasons.
I don't want to sleep in the afternoon shade.

Though I work harder, I tire so quickly.
Even if I rise up, even if I push Talus from the precipice,
he is born up, to become a partridge in the lower branches.

I am left to myself; sentenced to myself,
caring for my young, the brand of the bird upon my breast,
knitting wings for flight.

Preparing to start again, another journey,
people still depend on me. I am compared to younger men,
and have only my wits to rely on, my own company to ally.

Young men build their futures without the threat of failure,
assured comfortable lives. I can do nothing to unseat them.
I have begun so many times and cannot start again.

Still, I'm not ready to give in, to lie down.
Don't think I don't understand why I'm passed over.
I've forgotten more than they ever knew.

They try to instruct me.
They think I need their help.
They used to come to me to teach them.

I knew this day would come.
I understood clearly the way things worked,
but my strength is behind me.

Late autumn is here,
I wait for news from the doctor,
walls close around and winter snow coming.

Late summer raining,
    steamy afternoon weather
        wearing heavy clothes.

Relying on the White Queen

She was the white queen,
benevolent but commanding,
and he was her king,
moving in slow steps,
always to be protected.

They had been together
nearly sixty years
and weathered
so many things when
he was young and strong.

Now she's off to the next
appointment and visiting
grandchildren, pushing
him as he sits and wonders
where it all went and who

were those people he could see
in the back of his mind,
late when he couldn't tell
if he was awake or asleep,
or if it was really them.

He worries as she confronts
black knights and pawns
and he still knows her
his queen who sees to all
the white pawns that attend them.

She is devoted and if he falls
it is all over, it is all lost,
and she would not go on.
If she is lost, absent as he is
bishops and rooks would carry on.

He would still wander, one square
at a time, knowing that he
is vulnerable and she is gone,
and he doesn't care how many
pawns are forfeit or knights taken.

The game, however long, is over.

The Death of Venus

I saw them pull her from the water
blue eyes and lips and rippling tides
on the surface
soft light brown sandy bank
it smells like moss and crayfish
matted in her hair
and the corners of her eyes
blue eyes and soft light brown sand
low black wispy clouds, tails sip from the rippling surface
she watches without blinking away the sand
speaking water, breathing water without moving
blue eyes and lips and subsiding tides
I saw the spirit move upon the face of the deep
but not in the still blue ponds
soft light brown sandy banks
the thirsty clouds, with long black tails
cannot breathe and speak like she can
they cannot be so still
they veil charcoal skies in gray and black
and sackcloth and ashes
respectfully, the water and the skies, co-conspirators
seem pensive, almost penitent
as she lay so still on the sandy bank
her worn clothes draped about, here and there
a shadow of a Botticelli courtesan
reclining in the ornate salon of this late New England fall
or lying in state, her abusive lover looking on
we saw them pull her from the water.

Dark Sweet Cherries

I remember Hokkaido in cherry blossoms.
Though I never met all seven, as a child
I was pleased to know three,
boarders in our small home.

We were defended by the samurai.
As she arranged flowers at the table
he stood watch, spear in hand,
defending the sacred pagoda.

I wondered what the philosopher thought
as he watched me playing on the tile floor,
standing armies summoned from toy boxes.
I wanted to please him.

But Hotei I knew best,
laughing at the springtime.
He was easy to get to know,
always a part of games.

Would the wealth, longevity, and happiness,
I knew as a child,
content me now,
in the light of the full moon?

Leftover

After Thanksgiving dinner,
she says take some mashed potatoes,
and I can't eat all this pecan pie.
Is this your lid?

Then they hint,
you can leave some ham.
We pack up cranberry salad
but leave it on the counter

accidentally
falling asleep on the way.
I couldn't believe,
just since last time.

Still, she looked better.
I think it's the weight.
Did you see the baby?
The pictures took forever.

Even though he always
sleeps in the corner,
it won't be the same next year
without him.

The Face of the Waters

Swim in deep waters,
knowing what moves below,
how swift and powerful.
Feel the heat of the rising leviathan.

Hold still and hope to go unnoticed.
I am too weak to move,
so insignificant on the surface,
so lost on the vast waters.

Discarded in his wake,
as he breaches, I am swept away,
one soul lost at sea,
one soul lost in the deep of the night,

and the leviathan has no soul
and the spirit upon the surface,
the one soul, dividing,
and I've lost my bearings.

There is no lighthouse yet along these coasts.
There is no beacon piercing the night.
So tired, aimlessly I tread water
and if sleep should overtake me

neither leviathan, nor spirit, nor the night,
and I cannot imagine all that moves,
that hunts in the great deep.
Silently I watch for the first light.

Mother of Exiles

> Send these, the homeless, tempest-tost to me,
> I lift my lamp beside the golden door!
>> —Emma Lazarus, "The New Colossus"

I rise through adversity to find you.
Again and again I reach for your soft hand.
Silent lips cast your smile carelessly, demand
I follow, shameless, to your errand true.

Starched and pressed you draw other suitors too
who rise and fall along the course you've planned.
They lay desolate in your fertile land
while those who attend you, at last, are few.

A moth, I'm drawn to lamp by golden door.
Sanctuary, to live among your hosts,
yet scorched I fall and writhe upon the floor.

My past is future, and future nothing more,
fatal wounds from another teeming shore.
Mother of Exiles lights the way of ghosts.

Soneto para los Pobres

Pedro, Santiago, y Juan
are waiting for me to follow,
to bear the weight of the faith, hollow
in war torn hearts and lives, soon gone.

Santa Muerte claims the new dawn,
the faith of our mothers fallow.
Our visions now come from below,
Sangre de Cristo on the ground,

menor de estos, mis hermanos,
flows in thirsty barren acres.
All days, dias de los meurtos,

crops in savage storm remember
menor de estos, mis hermanos.
How blessed are the peacemakers?

September of 73

Salvador cut down,
crouching low in the palace
of the president,

> "By different means   to achieve,"
> bandits and messiahs all.

Realist Game Theory

So cliché, to recollect such unusual things,
so far away and so removed from my life.
I went to the north island as a small child,
with my father, mother, brother, and sisters.

So cold in the winter, so still and distant,
we went back in time. I was too young
to know, how the world had grown up,
peaceful places bathed in violent storms.

Not typhoons of summer, snows of winter,
but the wounded hearts and minds of nations.
Peaceful gardens and civil words worn as
ceremonial masks to an elegant dance.

Then we walked out onto the grey beach
one still and chilly afternoon to see them
among grey sands, grey skies, grey seas,
Jax as tall as elephants, skeletons resting

where they had fallen, concertina wire
garlands garnishing, along with kelp,
the smell of the ocean, defenses laid
beaches strewn with memories of war.

I asked as I climbed up from the wet sand.
They were on the beach to repel invasions.
Concrete toys, markers of unfought battles,
in defense of desolate beaches, forgotten.

We were a military family at cold war.
We had seen many memorials, parades,
tombs, remembrances of the fallen.
decorations and carefully folded flags.

Still, these markers remembered no bodies,
Or they remembered all of the bodies,
spread across the oceans and the continents,
foam caps so transient on the shifting sea.

Carlita Crossing Over

Carlita swam a different way,
slipped my hand,
in the dark muddy water.

In terror, I reach again and again.
Even slow currents,
could bear her weight away.

Under watchful eyes and a moonless night
she is gone,
my soul torn in half.

I must still my shrieking heart before they hear,
and work to draw the others from the river.
The water seems so thick on my face now.

I am almost blinded to the shore
and wish I could send them to safety
and cry out, searching
        until I hold Carlita's hand.

Deserving Poor

It is not some sweeping story from English literature
where the orphan, widow, or poor farmer suffers
tragedy and injustice,
left to beg, or shame, the cruel
efficient nobility
for tolerance and a stipend.

They stoop to glory in their charity,
all the while, careful to build character and teach.
A poor man can't figure out how to fish,
it couldn't be that the fish are not biting.
Luck alone cannot explain,
or if it could?

They, like you, could be outdoors, dispossessed
and could not save themselves.
But they are possessed,
capital and position,
left to preserve their station,
their vision.

What of happy endings, who was left?
Ever rescued?
It was hidden nobility or a stolen will,
not humanity,
that established their right.
Heroines often die, innocents in arms,
        carrion in the way.

We All Fall Down

Clasp hands as we spin around,
boys in a circle,
a game from my childhood.

It's hard to play with all this gear.
Hold on, don't let me slip away into the night.
The game is different now.

Still, we all know it will end in the wet grass,
all of us falling all around,
this time far more grim.

It seems the grass is full of snakes
and the mourning dew is blood.
Still, we hold tight.

The chanting from my childhood is silent,
though I heard most nursery rhymes are morbid,
some plague or wicked king.

Here the chanting is in our heads,
in unison,
faster and faster now.

If it has to be, we'd rather all fall down together,
and we try to believe we can hold on forever,
or at least until we fly away home.

While no one wants to be the first to spin off,
to leave the others short,
we're not sure we'd like to be the only one left standing.

We never played on foreign soil back then,
but we rushed into this game exuberant,
anxious for the thrill, something to do.

As I slip away, I call out for brothers and comrades,
"clasp hands, don't let go,"
but they follow me into the wet grass.

Even though we all fall down and the night close around,
we'll still fly away home,
in boxes draped with flags.

Civil Rites

Patriotism is martyred in waving flags
and void speeches, defending country
at the expense of countrymen.

The common good is become evil to the common.
Patriots do not care for the nation, for the state,
but for the people, for sacred lives.

We never found ourselves, patriots,
though we stood ready,
the rites were not administered in our generation.

We looked upon ourselves from the shadows
but we never met, never knew ourselves,
we never had the occasion.

Without the fire who knows the strength of the steel,
we bolted before we bore,
though it was a function of the season.

Still I'm sure we could have been noble,
gracious in our victories,
courageous in our martyrdom.

Are we better men for avoiding the conflict
never facilitating the flow of life into soft grass,
or casting souls into ambivalent breezes?

Immigration Policy

From broad seas we are gleaned;
    from distant lands we are drawn.
We sought no more than to be your lover,
    to hold you close.
On autumn nights we would draw your quilt around,
    would warm our little ones by your hearth.

But we see you from afar and dream of times
    when we can breathe free.
We have left our broken lives
    to stand beneath your bedroom window.
You leave on the lamp,
    but the golden door is bolted from the inside.

Though we buy you dinner discretely,
    you are ashamed to be seen with us in public.
Though we have honorably courted you,
    you lead us into a fool's paradise.
Found alone in your room, you denounce us as a robber.
    We flee from your garden window.

And return to the rundown apartment you pay for
    To await your letters.

Rwanda, and Kosovo,
and Somewhere in Central America

An empty sky, as far as I can see
cyan and wispy white and clear air
how silent it gets after they're gone

Three young men that have nothing
riding around in the back of the truck
while the man who owns the store drives

and they shout, and they throw things
bottles and rocks and hateful slogans
that they don't understand, but believe

and sometimes they get out and fight
with anyone they see, anyone with nothing
that reminds them of what others had

before that day when everything changed
everything spilled into the streets
and they left school and family businesses

and took what was theirs and what was not
and boys named for Moses and Saint James
and John the Baptist wash away their past

and their future in the blood of their neighbors
and priests that try to stop them
priests that try to keep children safe

while fathers and mothers are dragged out
under cyan skies onto gray streets
by boys who kick and swear and kill

by boys who will die when the soldiers come
or the rebels who ride in trucks and fight
for what was theirs and what was not

wispy white and clear air and birds that light
on priests and parents and children
not knowing them for who they used to be

Saint James forgets the time he spent singing
in the church on Easter and Christmas Eve
forgets the stoning of Stephen and how

they used to play on clear days with the girl
beneath the bird on the hot gray street
before he knew she was the cause, somehow

of the pains of a nation she had barely known
how her family deserved to be driven out
her clear-skinned shoulder embedded with gravel

and then they leave and it's quiet and still
and bakery windows are shattered into bread
drying in baskets, being eaten by birds

three boys die in an over-turned truck
burning and the man from the store seeps
into the street where they used to play

making bases from school books and teasing
the boy with the blotchy skin that grew up
and holds the rifle that claimed the man

left the truck unguided, rolling into the intersection
scraping arms and faces and legs and leaving
whispering wisps as the flames die down.

Release

Speaking of the revolution...
figuratively,
or the renaissance.

Death and rebirth,
samsara.

A revolution of arts,
the art of revolution.

Inquisitions, and Bolsheviks, and Sabine women.

Twisted, pained bodies,
torn clothes and the patina of death.

Epic stories in each model's eyes,
as if they had rehearsed their whole lives.

Naked man.

Far more than nude picnics in the French countryside
or Gauguin's utopia.

Memorials

How are people so impatient,
waiting for someone to take their order?
We love to visit historic sites
that those remembered, would rather have missed.

We take a picnic or stop at a café,
and read the plaque,
recalling brave soldiers and heroic struggles,
the sacrifices they've made.

Battles marched back and forth across farms
and cityscapes dotted with crumbled buildings.
Pleas came from camps where emaciated men and women
peered through fences looking for lost civility.

But sometimes I sit and wonder,
if I had been there at the time or seen from a distance,
would I have noticed where a small boy named Chaim
used to play by the garden wall?

A Cleansing Night

So clear, hear the flies in the night?
So distant, the lone crane takes flight.
Crouch low, move toward the open sky.
Up run hares and jackals in fright!

With the sun will arise a cry.
A village in ash paints the sky,
a smoky specter, an ill breeze,
calling souls of those who will die.

Shouted lust and hatred appease,
in crushing blows curtailing pleas,
overcome, I cover their ears,
run with them through vine shrouded trees

"Hold me and stay quiet my dears!"
Though trembling, I hold back my tears.
"Did she run? Is she gone ahead?"
I struggle to stand through my fears.

Unholy wars and mounting dead,
the innocents slain in their bed.
Yet no one will hear of our plight.
"Did she run? Is she gone ahead?"

Children of the Land

Fallow or alkaline I sit
a pariah
waiting for cleansing fire
and sweet rain
but in my day there is no planting
nutrient poor
absolute famine.

My strength unknown
my chastity lost
then trampled
by passing soldiers
then rebels
dancing to and fro
as my children go hungry
wanting.

At last war and famine done
the king is dead
long live the king
soon honor reigns with dishonor
a coalition government
and the water finally comes
new soldiers
find new rebels
and I am eroded.

I am fed by my children
they lay sleeping
trampled by passing soldiers
then rebels
pestilent nights
new diseases
and I have no power to heal
so I hold them close
torn by thistles roots.

Scattered

They came in from the deepest forest,
their lasting hatred burning before them.

Though she was a good mother to us all,
our home, she would have invited them in normally.

This time her tears flowed freely as she tried
to resist their improper advances.

Her children fled from her sheltering arms,
the home they loved, empty, consumed in shouts.

Then the torches and our vibrant home slumped
as an old woman racked with years lay down.

Soft rains caused the steam to rise from her heart.
Homeless, we watched her free spirit fleeting
while we were left with the revolution.

Long sleeves cover numbers
Other things I can't forget
Ashes in the wind

Civil Unrest

Gazelle feeding see
ripples move close through tall grass,
political winds.

Fleet egress leaves weak behind.
Lions fight over fresh prey.

  ***

Left along the way,
loved only by her homeland,
cradled in soft loam.

Perennial grasses dry
in scorching sun, unaware.

  ***

Laughing in the night
they hunt in packs, merciless,
even as she sleeps.

Children sitting in the dust,
the herd watches the night sky.

  ***

First they ask for names.
Then they tag us, track the herd.
Then trophy hunting.

Territorial lions
keep the hyenas at bay.

Ambivalent Exodus

Compassion and war
swept up in songs and marches,
settles into state,

and brutal bureaucracy
fierce wolves in Moses clothing.

Tens of millions here and there
in chains and fire and inhumanity
wait to see if she is here too, if he can make it.

They come in the night, or at work,
or when they're playing in the yard.
Who's minding the baby?

Administratively, there are papers and procedures,
it is efficient government
then they're moved to the next place.

Some places there is no process,
still there is order and planning to this chaos,
still efficiency in demolition.

Torn down, disassembled,
the edifices of the soul are defiled and left
to be swept up and hauled.

Where is he? Did he find friends,
not like they thought they had in the neighbors?
Who would care for him, hide him?

At last, their major concern,
will the land have the same loan value
with the structures razed?

There are lenders willing to overlook,
policemen who don't go
into some neighborhoods.

For some, nightmares and searching photographs
in the office, or on a wall,
the rest often lie together, edifices, or they're ashes,
        though they do not rest.

Surviving

He talked about digging the graves ahead
and looked around the clinic,
filled with families
and fragments of families.
She hid her child's face with her scarf,
as if I was death,
as if I wouldn't see him and he would live.

We left and walked along the dirt road,
back toward the cemetery
with the pre-dug graves,
and the small and large graves,
and the graves too shallow,
and people unknown except to ebola.

Ebola, who found them here,
running away from the city,
to this remote village,
where they had nothing left
now that they're gone.

A young girl kicked a ball
right past us,
into one of the open graves
near a gnarled tree,
and chased it
coughing.

We were leaving,
going home,
to families and children chasing balls,
to write stories,
and remember faces and people,
not the girl with the ball,
nor the hiding child and his mother.

The doctor who showed us around
went home to die in Cleveland,
where it didn't occur to anyone
except the lab tech and her family,
who gather around her in her room
and hoped for the best.

My wife and my editor keep asking how I feel.

Doves

There are always doves in the alley
They flee at my approach
Gentle creatures
Frail

I'm only trying to save a few minutes
I've hardly noticed them
Hurried as I am
Late

I cut through just to avoid the traffic
Risk their tender hearts
Morning suits
Souls

Passing through at a quick steady pace
Unconcerned with doves
Not a prowling cat
Waiting

I did not go looking for doves at all
Yet as they fly, they fall
Taken in the grill
Speeding

The Setting Sun

The drawing of the curtain,
the drawing of the night,
    and their dreams fade.

I saw my father slip into deep waters.
I saw him swim farther than he had strength
    and the lights dimmed along the shore.

My mother watched him slip away
and cried softly
    as he faded into his own eyes.

Winter Wind

In the winter wind,
heavy snows fall straight sideways
toward the western sky.

Filling work boots left outside
there is no one to wear them.

Apologetic,
I wonder if you see me
from where you're resting.

Until We Meet Again

He said "pray for us now and in the hour of our death,"
holding his father's rosary tightly.
When he returned home, she held him softly,
and they gathered their remaining children
and set a candle on the window sill.
They hoped their son could see the lonely flame.

"There is no God but God," she smiles with tears
and joy through the airy veils that protect her.
Her father's eyes fill with joy and sorrow.
Her mother could not see her shahada
and he must hold her with one arm
since that day in Palestine, that one day.

The mower shreds the wooden cross,
a passing driver swears as splinters hit the side of his car.
The man climbs down to see if he can put it back.
He wonders if this one was as young as his,
sixteen and her first time out on her own.
He can make out the name on the wood and remember.

He bows and leaves rice and fish and sake
on lacquered trays and in porcelain dishes.
The drums of Obon sound deep in his ears.
He leaves her a single chrysanthemum,
the sandalwood smoke reminds him of her,
one day he'll see her in the west.

They have a drink and tell stories of their childhood.
The perfume of the old women is too strong.
The children want to go play in their good clothes.
Now that it's begun in their generation
the siblings wonder who will be next.
She feels guilty for peeking behind the cloth.

They prefer to believe the wind is in on it,
the bending wheat and prairie grass
bowing toward the small plot and the open earth.
A few friends and the family and Brother James,
he would have wanted it this way.
The women have stew and bread at the church hall.

She is not here, even her ashes are gone,
released beneath the rolling waters far from here,
and farther still, her hands pressed in prayer.
He can still see her in red remembering him,
left behind, wondering where she is,
wondering if some part of her remembers him.

Three elders gather and dress him in temple robes
that no longer fit and say he doesn't look so different.
This is the first time for his eldest son to help,
to serve the dead, not far from here.
She waits patiently, knowing they are together now.
She can see their tiny child fall into his arms as he arrives.

He walks in the forest in recent growth, listening for voices
he cannot hear, voices of the chopped, haunting
the trees near his house, haunting the night.
His son was too young to be a soldier,
too young to be a rebel, too young to be so dead.
He offers kola nuts and fresh palm wine and tears.

A Delicate Craft

Swifts and swallows dart
through darkening stormy skies,
late season, fall rains.

Pressing engagements, or fear
of the dark in small frail skiffs?

Nothing is final,
though I thought you were at rest,
all bodies have ghosts.

Horsehide and string writhe
    empty on the grassy field.
        The ball is long gone.

Rest

What can death bring?
    Now that you've stilled my beating heart?
    Now that the thick hair of my youth is smoky wisps?
    Now that my joints are stiff and my steps slowed?

What can death bring?
    How can I fear blackness?
      Or stillness?
      Or undemanding quiet?

Will death sulk?
    If I find him ineffective?
    If I watch for him from the window?
    If I greet him with a kiss?

What will death bring?
    Debt consolidation?
    Free healthcare?
    Advise for the lovelorn?

Expectations

When my life is fled,
swaddled with cloth spun within
who prepared my shroud?

     In spider's web unto death,
     or cocoon, awake in spring.

Night Watches

In the night watches I look for the ghost of my father,
or the whisper of the Lord in my dreams.
I try to find form for the shadows in corners,
to see daylight in the darkest places.

Left to myself, I swim aimlessly in the thick fog,
calling out for the shore, listening for the bells at vespers.
I imagine a piercing beam in the shifting mists
warning me from treacherous rocks and jagged shoals.

As I reach out, I find your hand, hold tight
with last breaths gurgling from my lips.
Pull me from the unrelenting sea or pull the sea from me
and breathe the daylight into the darkest places of my heart.

Absolution and rest
I awake, at last, in a
broken chrysalis.

Ashes of Ghosts

It was 1944
and it was
secretive ash
ash confidant
collaborator
the structures
from one town
alone
charred black
crystalline cracked
and barefoot women and pigeons
picking
picking through ash
through whispers
through rumors of wars
wars
wars across
across homes and souls
souls swirling in the ashen wind
above char and regret
and barefoot women
alone
alone with collaborative ash
picking
picking through
through half-burned dolls
half-burned breadboards
and cats
ravening cats
looking on
twitching their tails
forgetting already
homes
charred
forgetting

watching the pigeons
watching the cats
cautiously
and cats grey with ash
and smudged with soot
licking but still watching
licking blood
from furry maws
trampling feathers stuck in ash
cats chased by women
but not away
circle and stalk
leaving grey footprints
wet ash on concrete
and sudden crashes
unstable structures
lump charcoal
falling discrete
and occasional hungry babies cry
muffled in conspiring ash
others lay quiet
tucked
blanketed
while women pick
calling
chasing away lean dogs
dogs that would not look away
cats that would not look away
discourteous
drawn
sniffing
women and pigeons circling
gathering their plumage
in swirling ash
through char-villages
and ruined farmsteads
too near
too far

barefoot women stepping
lightly
in secretive ash and charred walls
doors torn open
by violent flames
burned
and women in ripped skirts
and ash
ash
and soot
burned but calling
ignoring their skirts
picking
for food
for crying babies
and small children
left
accidentally
stained with ash
who saw doors torn open
and burned
they cried for women
in torn skirts
barefoot women
picking
looking
for babies tucked in and sleeping
so tired
picking
and there was rain that washed nothing
but cat footprints
and leaving dark grey
ash paste
and paint on faces
and clothes
and small children tucked in
still
sleeping still

tiny rivulets cracked ashen lives
drawing steam from timbers and studs
and greying coals
dying
and swirling ash settling
in hair
and torn clothes
with burnt edges
like old maps
with edges
and legends without true north
thorny crumpled compass roses
burned at the edge
frayed
ash ruffles
secretive ash
confidant and collaborator.

Waiting for Her

I hear summer drums.
Will you look in on me then?
Obon is coming.

> The cuckoo cried in the night,
> his voice in the western sky.

***

I took a long trip
driving along the seacoast
beneath the full moon.

> Still I miss those left behind.
> I love to see them playing.

***

It's time to go now.
Sail paper boats on the lake,
when Bon is over.

> Come and see me when you can.
> I miss you so much my love.

I have overcome,
now dress me for battle next,
or for final peace.

Resurrection

Our day was coming to an end,
bleeding into an otherwise calm sky.
We struggled to throw off the night
but our protests went unnoticed.

The still evening gave no hint
of the catatonic efforts we made.
The world is disconnected from us
our eyes dimming though we refuse.

As wisps of life, a hint of spice in the air,
we play upon the closing chilled wind.
we fade into the austere night and fear
though we expect the coming day.

I think I'll die,
so they tell me,
at first I thought not.

Choka and Tanka

Who will smooth his hair?
Do caterpillars wonder
what happens after?

    The chrysalis is wound tight
    and I am waiting for spring.

* * *

Who will read to him?
Epics of far away gods
tell of human fears.

    Their names on planets and months
    help us remember stories.

* * *

Who will show him snails
creeping along garden walls
leaving silver trails?

    Empty porcelain shells on paths
    that were not there yesterday.

* * *

Who will come and see
as he names the animals,
plays in the garden,

    before the fruit is ripe,
    before the animals bite.

* * *

Who will dress him up
in Sunday clothes and manners?
Grey owls sit and watch.

    I notice the moon fading
    as he watches for sunrise.

* * *

Who will let him eat
after he should be sleeping?
Cranes wheel in the wind.

    Sandhills so still in the sky,
    they seem pleased with the journey.

* * *

Who will hold him close,
though he rarely allows it?
Vines flee the lattice.

    Morning glories greet they day,
    wander from where they're planted.

* * *

Who softly wakes him
before the sun is too high,
and I have to rest?

    Snail shell in my woodshop,
    he'll have to clean it out.

Craft a paper boat,
sail it into the sunset
to see new places.

Vacancy

Short verses in the wind or lingering melodies,
waft through the vapid afternoon heat.
I walk out into what was a town and smell the decay
of leaves and livelihoods. Old buildings lined up
along a street too broad, like so many
ceremonial masks left over
from an abandoned faith or superstition.

The rails are no longer shining. Enameled
in the dark brown of oxidized time; they lay
across black ties oozing blacker creosote sap,
liquid in the still sunlight. Spikes are strewn about,
bent and thinned by years of rust.
Some can be pulled and pushed from hollowing cross-ties.
I pretend to great strength or the throne of England.

At such a young age I marveled at the hours
contained in each building or tool
or dislocated flower bed remembering
a revenant home or walkway. I pass quietly,
not wanting to wake the past, not wanting
to stir the curses that must attend such sacred ground.
I thought of casualties and intimacies among these ghosts
that tatted together a community so discrete and singular
in the expansive forests of the South.

I even came to think of my kinship to them
and my errant need to prove myself in their watchful eyes.
Feats of strength, acts of honor, signs of bravery, I was sure
would bind me to them, find me approved before them.
I idealized their ideal view of me.
I never considered that they might fall short of my standards.
That they were men rife with faults, never crossed my mind.

When I'm gone, I wonder, who will find my garden path,
or sift through my effects, to conjure up my ideal life?
What will they say I was, silently, to themselves?
Or will mine be one of those edifices, destroyed by fire,
remembered only by a line of daffodils too straight.

The cicada shell
clings to the side of the shed
no longer in use.

Tired

Replete, my soul sags under the weight.

I hear them say it all the time,
"I can't go on."
But I can't imagine how to stop.

"I wouldn't put up with that."
But there is nothing else
and nothing is unimaginable.

I am tethered to my life
and the world clings to my soul.

You look upon me and see my patina,
the aspect of my age.
Beneath I stand firm in my inertia.

But as you look past me
I tremble with decay.
Additions to my surface belie my crumbling core.

Though my provenance details my symptoms,
it gives no prescription.

One day I will shudder and fall.
When clamorous sound and billowing debris clear,
and I am laid open to all the world,

I will be scraped from the earth,
only to be interred out of the way.
What will I be then?

Reflections of Arlington

I crossed the river as a child.
An ornate bridge kept the way.

There I saw them, a library,
bound volumes as far as the eye could see.

They were a series on politics and poor diplomacy
and human nature.

They were identical to see,
an unbelievable amount to record on such a topic.

The covers carried similar information,
the text and quality of their prose diverged radically.

Other places, the faced does not favor,
the disparity of rich and poor is evident,
the love of others determinant, seen in their bindings.

Here there is uniformity.

The content, the plot
through twists and turns to a deliberate conclusion
a decided ending.

Then the formalities,
the family, the friends, or the appropriate agency,
summarize, endorse, or include the preface
before submitting the manuscript.

Then rolled and carried away,
the door closed,
the work bound.

The cover set in precious ground,
Flowers drink the tears shed by those who recall.

Intrigue

Summer rains on uncharacteristically still sands.
brief dark color, a blushing earth.
small streams cement themselves,
vanish in the diminutive landscape,
that stretches out of sight.

So quickly the blush is gone,
dragonflies land and try to drink,
from the thirsty land,
cheated by her false modesty,
uncharacteristically still, desiccated specimens.

Legacies

In the west, they are western.
In the south they are southern.
Back east they started the whole thing.

Their grandfathers built it,
bought it, founded it, planted it.
Their grandmothers had the best recipe,
quilted the best comforters, were the prettiest brides.
Their mothers could do no wrong.
Their fathers made this nation.

They have a different way of doing things down here,
which is strikingly similar
to the different way of doing things out here,
and around here.

* * *

We are another story altogether.

It's a shame our fathers and mothers didn't build anything,
didn't save,
didn't put away for a rainy day.

Sometimes we were there a long time;
sometimes we weren't anywhere a long time.

They don't understand, it was already raining.

They built it on our backs.
They bought it at the sheriff's auction.
They started it with our sweat.
They planted it in our blood.

Their recipes are made with quality ingredients;
not the spice of necessity.
Their quilts take time,
        a gift for those who need no comfort.
Their brides come from well paid tailors and photographers,
not intimacy and hope.

Our mothers could do so little, but so constantly.
Our fathers are the earth upon which this nation was built.

Their pedigrees are as clear as the streets
        and schools that bear their names.
Our families are scattered and our genealogies
        rooted in the murky waters of slavery,
        war, subjugation, and poverty.
We migrate, follow the harvest, hear of work,
        or are abandoned or retired along the march.
We didn't inherit; we didn't expect to.
We follow the rules
        and blame one another when it doesn't work.

* * *

The others took our jobs,
the others ruined it for everyone,
the others are too lazy, too shifty, too dirty,
        over-sexed, itinerate, and without ambition,
The others should be punished, fined, licensed, regulated,
it's what the others understand;
it's to protect the innocent,
it's to protect us all.

We believe it, everybody knows it.
Besides, it's our own fault.
We don't vote.

They may be right about the ignorance.
We honestly can't tell the difference between them.

Both of them have lofty plans
    to maintain us in our poverty;
out of the goodness of their hearts
and a sense of fair play.

But year after year they sell it and we buy it;
reluctantly, never realizing
we could grow it ourselves.
After awhile it's a religion with us.
When we vote, we vote the way our fathers did.

Who would have thought it could be so easy
    to choke to death on a meal without meat.

Someday someone will sell what we need,
    and it won't be a multi-level scheme;
or maybe we will just remember
that we are the earth and the blood and the sweat,
that form the foundation.

The foundation can move so slightly
    and the house crumbles:
but the foundation can support a new edifice.

I
A Proper Introduction

I've always had a strange relationship with Death.
Some people see death as a dark, hooded old man,
skeletal, grim, and grotesque, and always waiting.
I see her as a young woman, filled with passions,
sometimes kind, or curious, or jealous.

Death was, when I was young, tempted by me.
I was strong and able to attract attention,
and almost irresistible to death. Reckless,
I took risks; drove fast, climbed too high, lifted too much.
Death looked on as a would-be lover. She waited
for her chance to embrace me, to hold me tightly.
Her advances, while exciting, could not take me.
Still, I was ever aware of her attentions,
the scent of her perfume hung in the air.

As I grew older, I saw her vindictive side,
as she taunted young mothers, calling their children,
and isolating the elderly, so hopeless.
I heard the rumors of her illicit affairs
with husbands and fathers at war, so far from home;
and her vengeful behavior among the children,
the children of the poor and of the powerless.
Even the rich and well-placed could not find safety.
She was just as cruel with the wicked as the just,
claiming them all with equal callousness,
the first born of Egypt and the last of Darfur.

Later, as I grew to understand her better,
I thought I could see her motives and her passions
as she lifted the starving infant to her bosom
and whispering so softly, she stilled his sobbing
and put him to sleep. I wondered what she whispered.
Then it was clear, as if the child were her own,

she spoke gently of the coming dawn and sweet days,
if he would just close his eyes and quietly rest.

Can she be the careless tart and the sainted nurse,
the vicious conspirator, passionate lover?
Does her repertoire include the liberator,
singing songs and shouting slogans and promising
an unprecedented freedom from brutal war?
Once she is enshrined by an indebted nation,
can she crush the opposition without regard,
kleptocratically stealing all she can steal
without a thought for her former comrades?

Surely her many moods and faces are varied,
as varied as the venues in which she performs.
Her make-up and wardrobe, it seems, change with her roles.
Often she is type cast as the brooding villain.
She's seldom cast in the role of the heroine,
and then she's only revealed late in the plot.
She is a single woman, villain, heroine,
with her many avatars and emanations
enshrined in ceremony and rite, worshipped.
She is ignored, she is denounced, and she is feared.

One thing I cannot believe is the cold reaper,
or the purely instinctual tigress hunting
in the night without affections, dispassionate.
No, I see her, smoldering, or raging, complex,
and deeply intimate in her relationships.
I see her living with passions, crippling regrets,
regrets for the dirty work that is hers alone.
I see her moved and weeping at the fears,
the fears that she cannot allay in her charges.
But I cannot be certain that she, the tigress,
does not also relish the hunt.

II
The Shadow of Death

Sometimes she does not kill, but lingers near, flirting,
coyly terrorizing her acquaintances.
This is clear in the eyes of the widow, pleading,
or geriatric patients clinging to their life,
clinging to what they almost remember.
She's a close friend, an avoided debt collector.
She is a dance partner who has, regrettably,
already promised this song to another.

We worry about her influence as we see
her leaning in and whispering intimately,
speaking in hushed confidences to our loved ones.
She plays children's games with my grandmother so soon
after such an encounter with my grandfather.
I remember working in a hospital ward
while the white-haired veterans sought her company
or were led unknowingly into deep waters,
feeling horror and tasting the salty sea,
or mistaking her for their dear mother or wife.

III
An Agent of the State

She is often endowed with the seal of office.
As an agent of the state she can, with clean hands,
or dirty, administer the passing of souls,
the fomentation of unrest. Deliberate,
here she is bureaucratic, skilled, and punctual.
Technocratically, she closes her case files;
she sends her staff into civil societies
to clear her desk. Dispassionate,
this is her most troubling persona.

Bureaucracy can be a stark environment,
too officious in the best of circumstances.
Gross expenditures in The Department of Death,
the Infant Mortality Assurance Bureau,
approved under the auspices of her office.
Here she can, for the greater good, destabilize,
promote social class struggle, and prosecute wars.
She can effect exclusionary policies.
With feigned affection she removes children from homes
and sets prudent immigration criteria,
punishes or rehabilitates the wicked,
executes the paternal judgments of the court.

She sleeps well after a day's work, comfortable
secure in the knowledge that policies are met.
She brings greater efficiency to government,
A career bureaucrat, she's without compunctions.
Her lack of party affiliation assures
appointment across many administrations.
I see her in this role sometimes tired, callous,
and underpaid, or idealistic, zealous.

IV
Cleansings and Pogroms

Sometimes Death stirs the masses, or the few;
she feeds them on the scraps of their countrymen, chum,
blood and flesh in the water. Some cannot resist
power at any cost. Yet, some cannot forgive
even the most unintentional offender.
She is prepared to protect their rights, to evict,
to exact damages, and to see justice done.

She enjoys, at times, fame, and anonymity.
She has always held many posts in government;
she has held many posts in the insurgency.
She is the voice of purity and tradition,
and she is the voice of change and liberation,
the poet, sweet poisonous words in willing ears,
the lover, leading nations in torrid affairs.
Exhausted and swept-up as they are in passions
she devours them as the black widow.

Though she is a modest girl by nature, she was
put on exhibition in the Roman Circus,
openly ravaged at the Bastille.
She's always been sought out by a certain type of man
who did not care for her virtue, or discretion.
She has been sold and forced into prostitution
in interim courts of itinerant justice.

She is mocked and put to shame before jeering crowds.
More of a public figure than she would prefer,
her name weaving in and out of the news. She finds
her loves and heartbreaks in the society page
and her subtle whispers are reduced to lewd acts
in the entertainment section. She is exposed
by the upright for her wonton indecency;
upbraided by the pious for what she has done.

In this emanation, objects of her hatred
or objects of her affection do not fare well.
As the Stygian pilot, she will be paid.
As revolutionary, or saint, or soldier,
she feels the fiery righteousness of her cause.

When wars rage and revolutions lie, in times of sacrifice
and vengeance; when it comes time to cleanse a nation
or punish the small children of an enemy,
the only question lingering is: who is she?
Does she play the part of the dog of war hunting
in the wafting smoke, or the battlefield nurse
alleviating the suffering of the dying,
spiriting away the infants not fortunate
enough to find small boats in bulrushes?

V
La Donna è Mobile

Sometimes Death is just another actress, waiting
in the wings, watching and listening for her cues.
I wonder if she feels trepidation, stage fright?
She chooses her delivery and stumbles through.
Her lines are well rehearsed, her blocking is practiced.
She gives a convincing performance or falls short.
Backstage we know her as any other player.

So often she changes costume, so many roles.
Sometimes she is a mendicant street performer,
the woman inconstant like a feather in wind.
She gathers withered wildflowers for her role
as Mercutio's shadow laughing as he falls,
or the implied consort of Mephistopheles.
More often she is a shadowy character,
essential to the plot. Without her there's no crime.
Without her the stage would fill with roleless actors
in plotless melodramas. The world is her stage.

VI
Death's Door

They say we begin to face our mortality
in our thirties or forties or when we lose someone .
I think we see her clearly when we are alone.
I saw her first when I was a child, a glimpse
through a window, a stormy night. She visited
my home as I lay in my bed in the dark room.
She did not leave alone, she never leaves alone.
I heard the sobbing down the hall the next morning.
Later she came to me in unsettling dreams
in shadowy corners of my room. I recall
her following me for blocks on very dark streets
coming home from an eerie movie by myself.

We never really lose sight of her once we have
someone to miss. When someone slips away from us,
from family gatherings, we look around to see
her missing as well. We wonder where they get to.
Who will she seduce next? Who will she call her love?

We all see her face-to-face sooner or later.
Overprotective mothers warn and tell folktales,
while young lovers plan to visit her together
in the fall when they will have enjoyed the summer
but arrived safely before the first winter snows.
But not all lovers are young, some plan an evening,
a snowy walk, before curling up together.

VII
Our Legacy

What monuments men build. As she takes my rough hand,
leads me down unmarked paths, through dark thick forests, I
wonder at the advice of clerical ravens,
standing in black suits interjecting warning words
or instructions. We slow among the lush foliage,
so dark green it becomes lost in shadows, and she
presses her soft hand to my face. She speaks to me,
promises to cherish my memory.

How is it she leaves the sweet memories of some
and removes others root and branch? What mementos
will she collect? What memoirs left to my loved ones?
I seek a legacy that will tie me to life,
the living. For many this is life eternal,
to be remembered. Forgive me, I paraphrase.
Yet I contemplate my stature in their eyes,
the bereaved, and I consider what they will say,
what will they tell the bees when I do not return.

VIII
Honored Guests

Sometimes it's not Death, but the dead, who are so close,
so present in our lives. Everything reminds us
of the dead, keeps them close, in our thoughts and homes.
They watch us patiently from her shadow, hiding
behind her skirts. Surely they, and she, cannot be
far off. Surely the veil between us is not thick,
not impenetrable. Are they aware of me,
as I am of them? I wonder what he would think,
what my grandfather would think. We imagine them
how they would look, how they would see us, if
they were still here, alive I mean. How we miss them.

Some never played or took their first breath, never woke.
What thoughts they must have held locked within, unable
to speak them. They waited so long to come, and then
they waited alone in their room until she came.
She bore them away, precious infants in her arms.
We imagine how they would look if they were here.
And though we never knew them well, how we miss them.

We rest assured in our faith. In eternal plans
we cannot completely understand. We affirm
our convictions that they were more valuable there,
safe from this world, too perfect. Maybe it's their time,
so soon, maybe it was best this way after all.
Always we rely on the happy scene of them
falling into the arms of loving ancestors
and others gone that way when they arrive.

Though they are gone, we are haunted, or watched over.
Sometimes they are just not that far from us, from here.
We feel them, or remember birthdays, or hear tunes,
so briefly catch the smell of his pipe, of her hair.
Either way, Death keeps them close to us as she hints
at our reunion and reminds us of that veil.

IX
My Part

I don't know exactly how I feel about her.
She is exotic, passionate. She captivates
my imagination, though I do not trust her.
I could never embrace her, yet she pursues me,
and sooner or later, I acquiesce.

I wonder, what my part is, and what role I play.
If she offered her hand, would I dance, and kiss her,
and kiss her ring, and honor her station? Could I
run to her for the noble cause, or find honor
or dishonor as her agent? Soldiers and spies
dance as bees in the hive for everything worthwhile.
Physicians fight to drive her back valiantly but
in vain, or sleep as derelict guards at the gate.
Bishops comfort and parents reassure.

What role do I play, or what role should I have played?
Does she court me to be close to those close to me?
If we are not as well acquainted as others,
she and I, am I as honorable? As strong?
As courageous? Can I be quite as heroic,
the dispassionate servant, or am I her prey?
Even in her absence she is present.

X
Waiting

I recall as a young man sitting down outside
the station, almost midnight, waiting for the bus.
Unsavory travelers turned their attention my way
from time to time and I could ruffle my feathers,
could send them on their way without confrontation.
Nevertheless, as the cat's eye catches her prey,
the epilogue is already written.

Some seek her out, extend their open hand, and bow,
while others avoid her gaze, explaining to her
they cannot dance. "Come" she insists. "I'll teach you."
The courtesies make the dance so much more pleasant.
There is no real point in dreading the encounter.
In time there will be one dance beneath the full moon,
a peaceful end to an eventful day.

We have courted from time to time over the years.
She's no good at long term relationships.
But like cats and birds, sooner or later we dance.
Some seek her. Some fear her. Some deny she exists.
I've simply grown accustomed to her company.

The Viewing of the Dead

Sleeping in his suit he looks so natural,
almost a receiving line,
like a wedding or some diplomatic reception,
except he doesn't shake hands.

We are water carried in earthen pots,
or black ice in the encroaching afternoon.
Still, everyone gets a turn,
though sometimes no one comes to see or wants a turn.

If he has something more to say,
it eludes me. He no longer has the floor,
even if the gathering is held in his honor.

The viewing of the dead is such a personal thing.
We step up one-by-one, lean close and whisper
or stay at arm's reach.

No one sings or prays aloud or speaks on their behalf here.
We just file through,
or not, and remember,
        as pottery shards crumble into fine powder.

With Very Little

She crouched outside stones with coals in their care,
seasoned steel,
seasoned hands,
experienced at conjuring flat bread
from turning oil and sparse meal.

Tortoise looks on and laughs,
not to be trusted.
She helped him to the feast,
waited her turn,
but came hungry to the village.

Children cradled in her arms,
swaddled on her back,
she strained to lift them from reach of following dogs,
took care to find them a place to sleep,
as forest shadows marked her path.

Inside, voices,
thick with palm wine,
kola nuts, and bargains around warm hearths
from close compounds,
mock her single hut.

Orphan, widow,
mother of the dead,
is there one name for all?
Or without, is there a need for names?
Remaining young ones, only cry   or laugh unaware.

Sometimes pleading with tortoise for understanding,
sometimes warning shadow demons
or dodging their gaze,
then she's lost in their eyes
their grasping hands around her finger.

Hoeing yams as they play in the grass,
weaving hut and basket,
trying not to attract help
in brutal company.
In a few endless seasons her young steady her .

In a few more short ones,
they build their huts,
remember her
as she remembers what it was to lie beside him, before,
and other children playing at the feet of grandparents.

As she slips off her clothes,
she chides the tortoise
stands boldly before shadows.

Her strong sons make their way,
and remember the mother of the dead.
She watches proudly,
they feed her palm wine, kola nuts with flowers
in a beautiful basket on the ground.

Abel

There are names that only we know,
shrines, sacred only to us,
gardens watered by our tears
　　　along the way.

They are seldom mentioned,
some only once.
Too soon and too late,
　　　unanswered.

They must be remembered for a lifetime,
lifetimes,
and more,
　　　silence.

Where do they rest?
Where do we,
and for what?
　　　What labor waits?

Among templed roots they swim,
torn down,
not one stone upon another,
　　　far from here.

Lifeless?
Names whispered in the branches,
through bare autumn limbs and sweet gum balls
　　　that refuse to fall,
　　　in the face of winter winds.

In the spring they're rebuilt,
beautiful shrines,
three days,
　　　or more?

Awakened,
names spoken aloud,
still hard to hear,
    muffled by deep embraces.

Keepsake

As we moved, I took the photographs from the wall,
as we always did.

We boxed the old clothes to give away,
moved the furniture from her room.

Gathered the toys, the drawings,
the fragile doll had been wrapped in a clean cloth,
placed in its own wooden box.

We wept as it was loaded,
though she would play with it again.

One

Children buried from cancer wards,
or UNICEF commercials, feel the same.
Mothers sobbing in waiting rooms
or refugee camps, red eyes and disheveled hair.

Crying in the night, left alone
in suburbs or alleys, broken homes,
blows and words and shattered trust
slipping, hiding, and explanations.

Stooped and sore and dimming eyes,
strained at simple tasks, or thoughts,
rain upon the just and the unjust,
a common lot, and finally, dressed by others,
        loved ones or officials.

Still

Subtle night is still shelter
from the beating hail,

and glaring sun,
without voices and riddles.

Merely a breath
and robbed of life.

Taken in the den,
never to draw.

The soft breeze,
the eternal currents.

To Plait Celestial Chains

They also serve who only stand and wait.
            —John Milton, "On his Blindness"

They also serve who only stand and wait.
Ere even days in this dark world and wide,
small souls, or large, peek into this estate.
Then side by side, their errand to confide.

Bound firmly through celestial veils to plait,
complexly braided chain not set aside.
If each will do honor to his own state,
then together into the light they stride.

So sits the hopeful, final state of man.
So depend the living on the dead, yet
ancestors and children stand together.

Watchful guides as we pursue Gods great plan.
Gone on, or yet to come, can we forget
the reward, when on that shore we're gathered?

Childhood

Black and white television took us to the Ho Chi Minh Trail
and the Sea of Tranquility
the May Day parade at the Kremlin
and the Eternal Flame

A dull brown Rambler wagon took us to the Cumberland Trail
and Arlington
protesters on the Pentagon steps
and the Tomb of the Unknown Soldier

A modern brick chapel took us to the strait and narrow path
and silent rites
the congregation on Christmas Eve
and the communion table

Deep End

She believes
and dives deep into the blue.
Chlorine smells clean the air.

I can lift her, hold her,
dive for her, to protect her
from so much.

I cannot swim
and my life will have little effect
to save her here.

Ecclesiastes

Whether conscript or volunteer I cannot say
from dim memory past,
but alas, we are off to the fray,

There is no discharge in that war.
We are oft bested,
and when tested, suffer afflictions sore.

Sooner all fall by the way,
none are exempt and
though they win or lose the day,

all die and fail, the preacher warns.
Though we slay the beast
we are caught on ivory horns.
And whether life be war or feast,

all stand to account.
For our time in life's raging stream
we are saved by paltry amount.
Deserving, he only can redeem.

Ravens follow me
they are waiting as I age
for some birthday cake.

Vigil

Still darker was the night
than any I had seen before,
and she rested
while I laid awake
and stared
waiting for the terror.

Surely it must breach placid waters
to snatch me into unspeakable pain,
or perhaps
the stillness of her absence
is enough
to terrify my heart
on into the vague;
no, certain.
I will follow, after
what seems a lifetime.

I expect to arrive
winded,
disheveled, in a cold sweat
as a child from a nightmare
and crumble into her arms sobbing.

Men I Met Along the Way

When did I say who would carry me home?
Old men, and ways, include me and I go
to see through old eyes and values fallow.
Secure in their borrowed strength I have flown.

My back bends as theirs and my spirit groans
I find myself moving in time narrow
tame from the load, I pull to the cargo,
to the task worn and to the lattice grown.

Already down the path unwitting led.
The old way does not lead to new places.
My lust to find their self-respect is fed.

As I strive alone to see my piece said
the feeling creeps across my heart with dread,
in the glass, grave terror scars their faces.

Early Harvest

We trail from the field,
mud caked in the arch,
our footprint broad with it
and hard to leave.
Slipping in the thick earth,
it stiffens our pant legs.
We pack soil to us as the potter
before we are turned.

Grabbing what produce we can
as we are beaten by the driving storm,
our cool sky turns angry toward us.
The earth around us
suffers for harboring us
and gives us up to greater force.

To our meager shelter we are confined,
pinned down and taking on water.
In our heart and lungs,
the breath sweet in our nostrils
cannot be breathed deeply enough
to overcome the load we carry.

As though we were too close to the medusa,
we are scathed.
We try to shed our cast
to leave our death mask shattered in the bare floor;
but we have not for our needs
and our dying garden cries.
We see our lives being washed,
scoured from the earth so that it can heal cleanly.

Into the slick ground we wade
falling and tumbling, grasping for leaves,
pulling a few tubers from the softening earth

like catching fish with our hands.
Most of what our muddy hands can hold
will slip away
through our silty fingers
before we can get it indoors.

Rains pass through us
to our most secret parts,
stripping away our most modest defenses.
We are chilled through
humbled for all to see.
Our souls abandon their outer perimeters.
Even our flesh tries to fall back.

Discrete we find ourselves
fighting the blindness
that washes over our eyes
in heavy waves and locks and mud.
Our stinging eyes fight for air
as we slip into the growing deep
and desperation,
and what direction we can find
cannot be trusted.

Some see no real danger here
as we breathlessly fall to the floor
and peal the layers
striving not to break free from our chrysalis',
but from our shrouds.
Heaped together, our severed clothes
bleed a fine alluvial brook into the floor boards.
Fresh wrapped, we wash the fruit of our labors
and they dwindle in the chipped sink.

Though their bright colors begin to show through
and we begin to hope,
still they shrink in the flowing water
and shed the earth to expose malnourished forms.

Taken prematurely,
greens are yellow and bright colors, still green
and though we have sown,
we can feel the hunger already.

Time upon time
lays heavy on our shoulders
and we read no special meaning
into the coming light.
The scourging rains leave us
to the sterilizing steam and vivid colors
that some find a symbol of hope.

We are not so quickly convinced
as we have been taken in,
played for a fool before,
against our will,
and left the sadder for it
with no degree,
no trade good,
to establish the wisdom gained.
We look upon our small harvest,
so hard won, too little, too late.

Sullen, we sit at meat
feeling guilt, and planning
for the next season,
while others think we do not understand
the folly of our course,
we cannot quite convince ourselves
of its merits, of our performance,
but we must pretend and act and assume
some ever lowering standard of success.

As the growing ice destroys our stores
and the masked rains begin to fall
in huge white flakes
to camouflage the dangers

of the icy road and sing
seductive songs to our childhood senses,
we walk unbundled into the still grey air
searching the cracking ground beneath our feet
for some manna we may have missed.

Which am I, locust
in sweet breezes flown, or left
exoskeleton.

Memorial Service

Death comes sometimes as soft as a gossamer strand
on the nighttime path, or as hard as the crescendos
of crushing trains colliding and falling from their tracks.
In all the clamor, in all the details, we're left to wonder,
which sound is the soul slipping from the temple of clay?
If we are death's quarry, does all sound stop suddenly?

Our mortality will be greeted with casseroles in church halls,
expressions of surprise at how much they've grown,
and honorary mentions of those closest, in printed programs.
None of which, it seems have the power to recall the dead.
The casserole with the chilies, sour cream, and bacon is close.

The occasion is marked with clichés and common greetings
traded in comforting corridors of churches and mortuaries,
by people who should have known each other better,
or not at all. Depending on the circumstances,
on the former health and spiritual status of the deceased,
we decry death as a predator or celebrate the angel of mercy.

The occasion is an invaluable institution for mending walls
and updating address books with familial synapses
that will never fire. Each generation looks as we remembered
the last, from twenty years ago at Uncle Charles' funeral
where the preacher pronounced a summary judgment
        in order to unburden the higher court.

From Somewhere in Africa

There is blood with bone slivers
drying on the porch rail, and children's toys,
scattered and crushed beneath boots in the night.
A woman with her life coagulated
in the hollow behind her ear,
lying in the morning sun, nursing thick green flies,
so quick to find her. There is a man tangled
in the fence, his fists clenched, silently clinging
to a shovel, and burned so thoroughly that the flies
don't see him. He was poised to stave off soldiers
and militiamen, that were neighbors, grocers
and teachers and firemen last month, upset
about the economy, and today they are war criminals,
driven from their homes by peacekeepers,
peacekeepers who were always soldiers,
who can't believe what they see,
or what the deep whispering forest tells them
about the darkness.

Snow Angel

We used to lie still in the snow,
staring at the late afternoon,
getting lost in the steel-grey skies,
completely losing track of time.

I turn my back to falling snow,
accustomed to the afternoon,
hurrying home under dark skies,
always aware of fleeting time.

Why could we never feel the cold?
I miss those silent afternoons.
How long since we looked at the sky?
We should forget about the time.

    We ought to lie still in the snow.
    We should get lost in steel-grey skies.

Beyond the full moon
  lies a new crop of blossoms,
        the scent of her hair.

The Potter's Field

Driven, as we were, from the homes we loved,
and those we did not,
we found ourselves wandering, far from our plans,
far from our nativity.

Trained to the trellis, we should have known better
than to wander away.
I should have known better, should have listened
to foreboding voices.

Not once only, not rarely, if I shouldn't have played there,
why was the street so wide?
Why did we spend so much time as children, learning
how to cross, then how to drive?

At first a wilderness is a picnic, then an adventure,
then the potter's field.
And following friends into the graveyard, how can I,
with wide eyes return?

How can I not see the beauty of the sepulchers,
designed to please the eye?
Designed to make serious, foolish lives, and to make fools,
wish for death.

So in streets and cemeteries and in darkening forests
I wander, I play, I lose my self.
I forget the way only for brief moments here and there,
then dusk settles between there and home.

I am not in danger of freezing or feeding ravening wolves,
or finding a blade in my back.
No, so much subtler is the hand of death, so cunning,
as I descend into the dark earth.

Lying down in the grave, only to rest, I find myself
staying too long, losing track of time.
Only late in the day do sunbeams reach me where I lie,
and I am past waking.

In the garden path
snake's skin, for the new season
not loss for the old.

Northern Sea Circuit

In Hokkaido
where I spent my childhood
deep snow everywhere,

> surrounding even the young
> though I never got too cold.

A Single Silver Claw

Slip-moon sailing
Sails furled failing
Slicing falling skies
Single claw, clawing
Dawn-tide rolling
Washing warm morning
Over grey haze
Hazy night harboring
Slip-moon sighing
Sailing into dawn

Holy War

I guess it all started with Sarai and Hagar.
When the hospitality of Canaan wore thin.
Coveted wells and abused groves, dotted
the promised land. And Moses, poor Moses,
blamed and praised and forgotten except in name,
cries before the congregation still. Cries
for the wounded child; weeps for the wounded people;
cries for the wounded land, forced to bathe
in the blood of her young ones. Colonies and crusades
and caliphates and resettlement,
devour the manna saved for Shabbat.

Now it's like any other day. Bought and sold
and pressed into service, while stone tablets
are ground into gravel for roadways lined
with soldiers. Not soldiers following the Arc
or fleeing chariots across the seabed,
but soldiers. For the eids and the feasts
and the holy days, the olives are pressed
with heavy hands and the heads of the weary
are anointed with the blood of noncombatants.

God, drawn like a sword, or the stiletto
of robbers and assassins, cannot sit by.
Sooner or later the landlord will be paid.
Sooner or later the fire will issue from the censors
and consume the children of Kolath.

www.ingramcontent.com/pod-product-compliance
Lightning Source LLC
Chambersburg PA
CBHW022012090426
42741CB00007B/999